A Pond

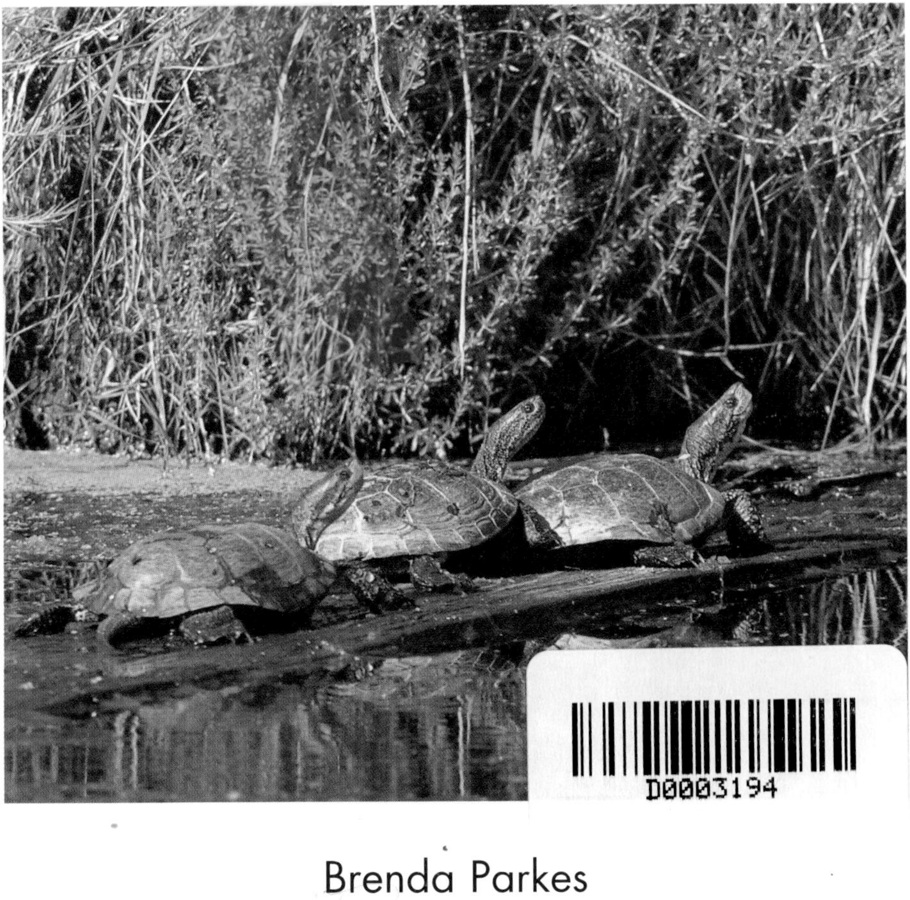

Brenda Parkes

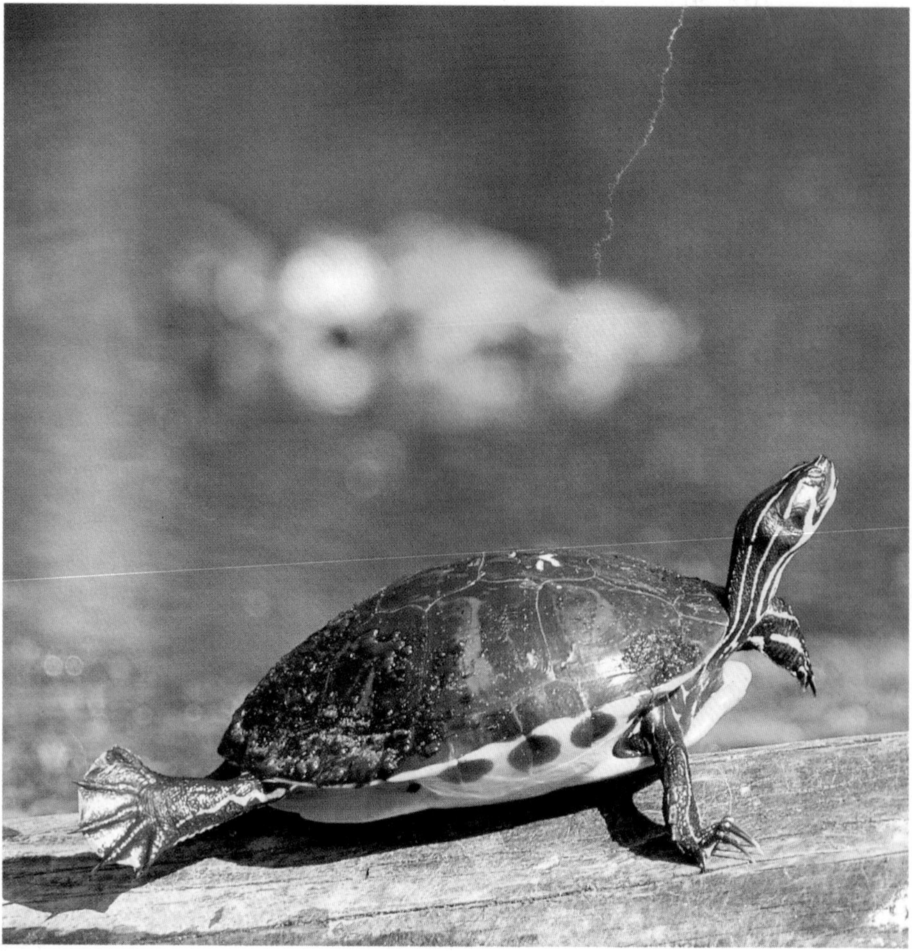

A turtle,

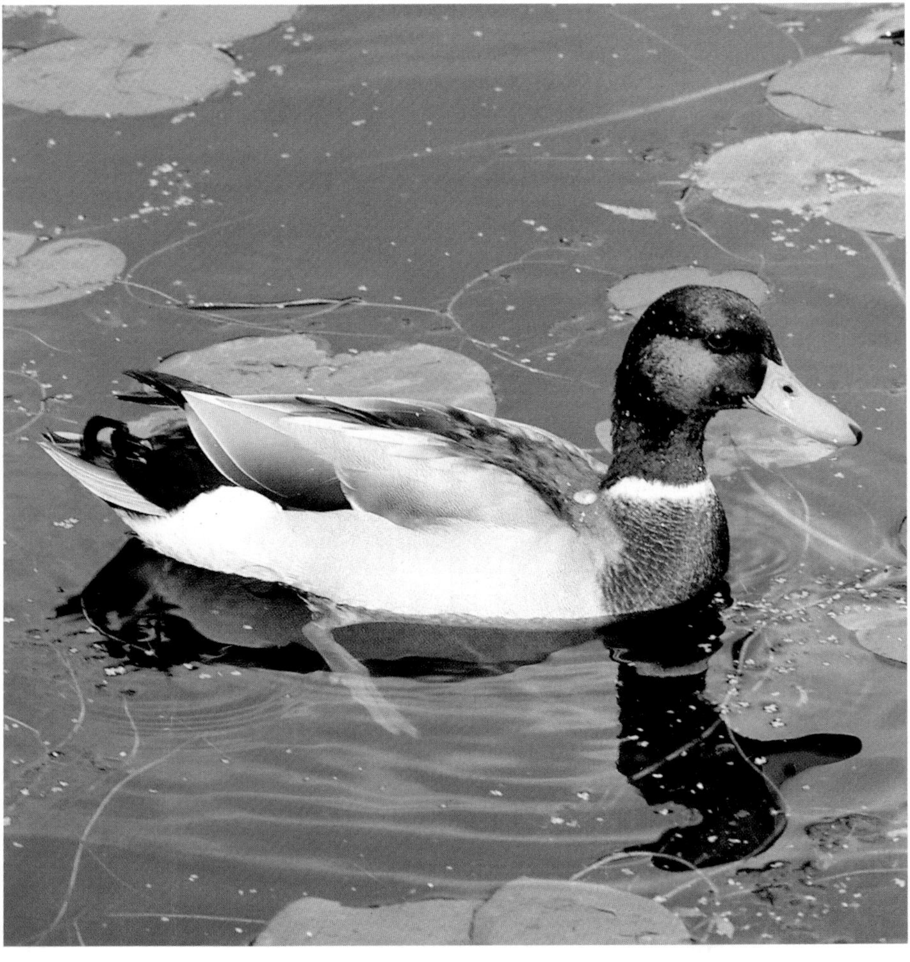

a duck,

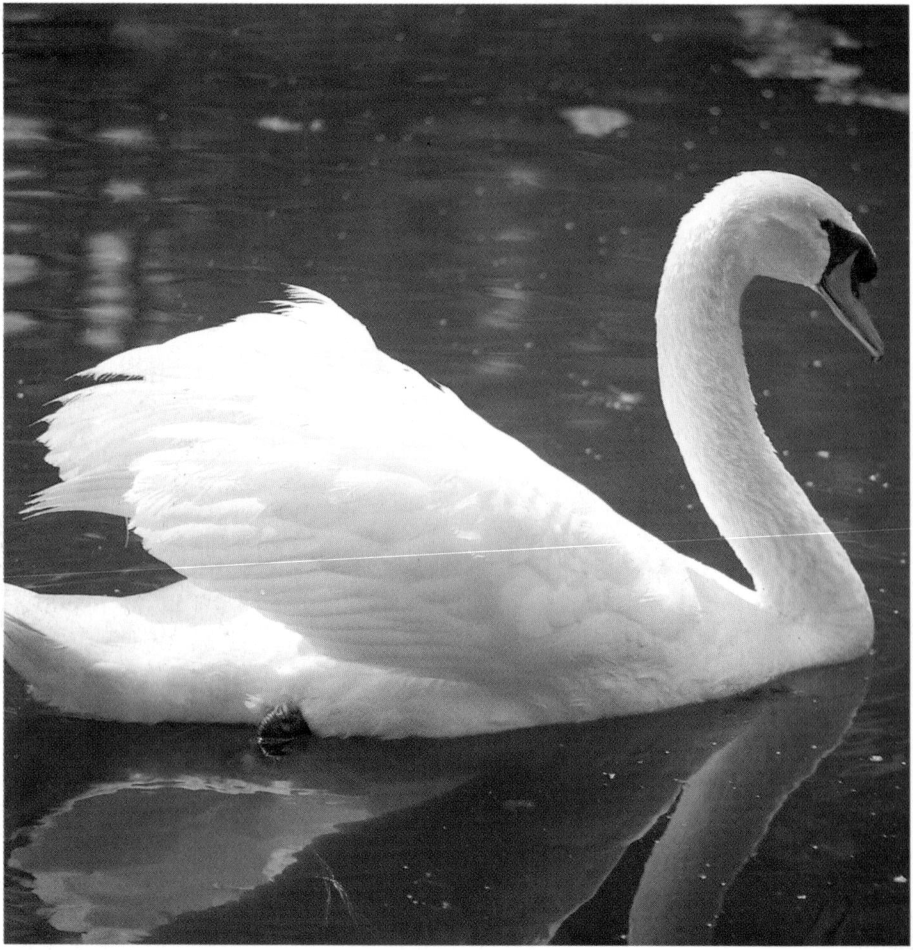

a swan,

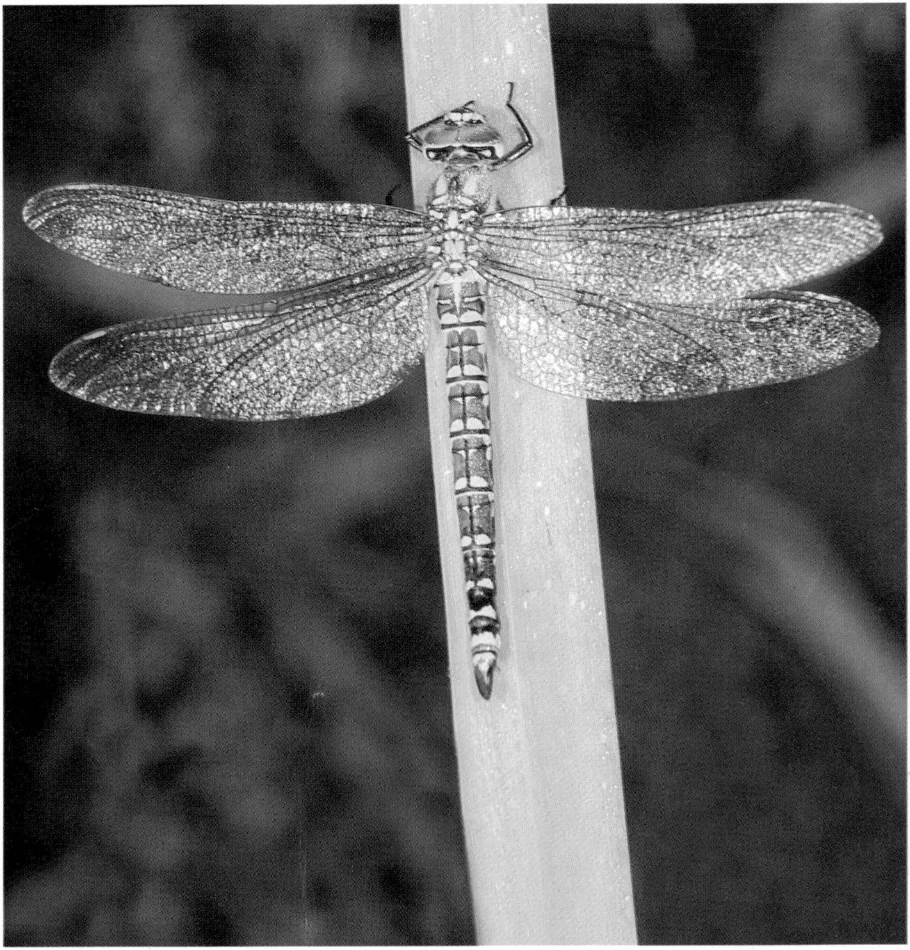

a dragonfly,

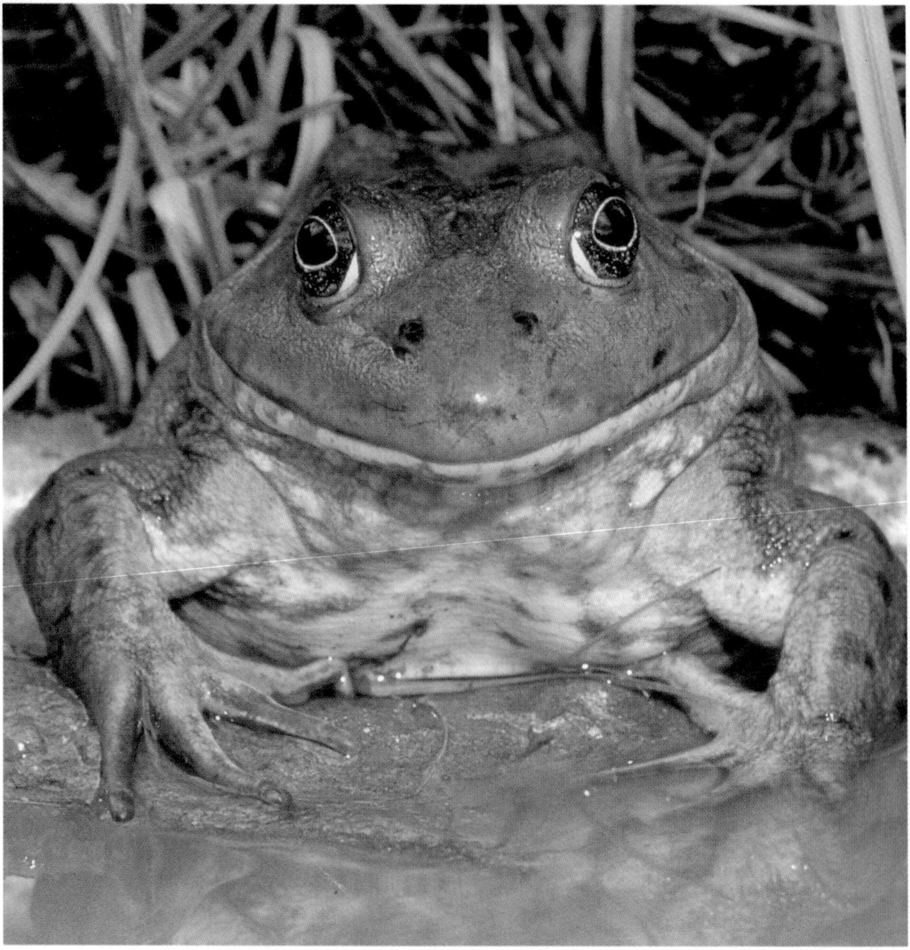

a frog,

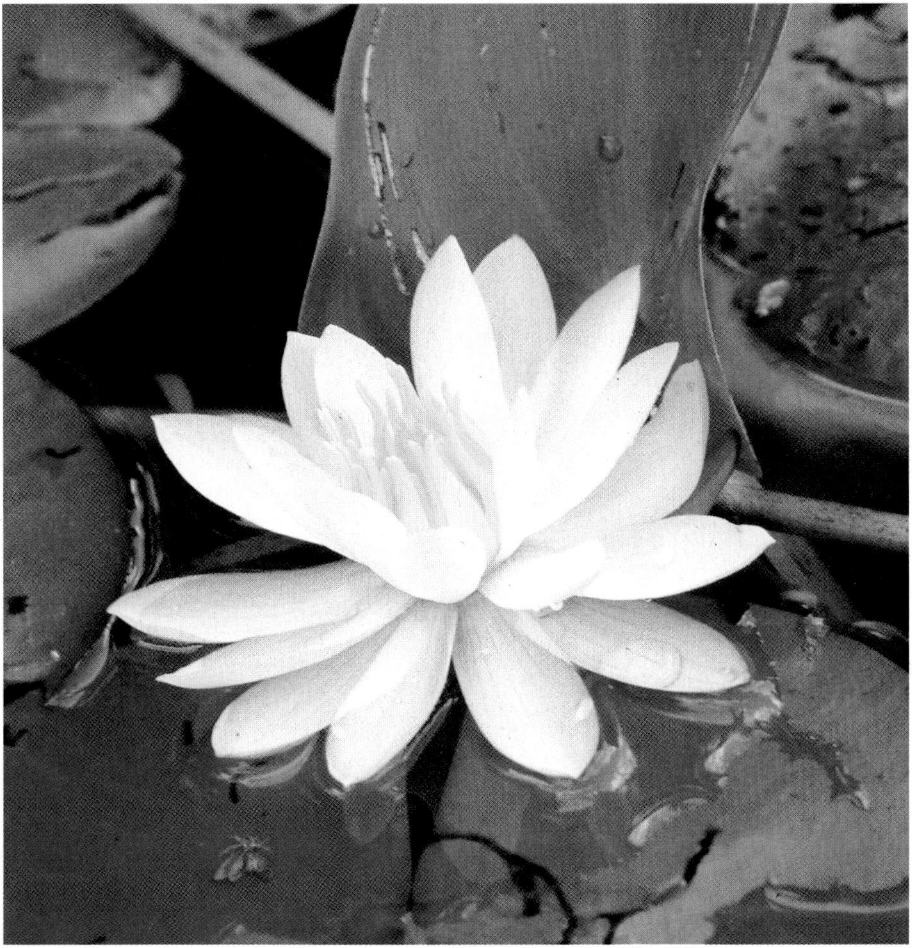

a flower,

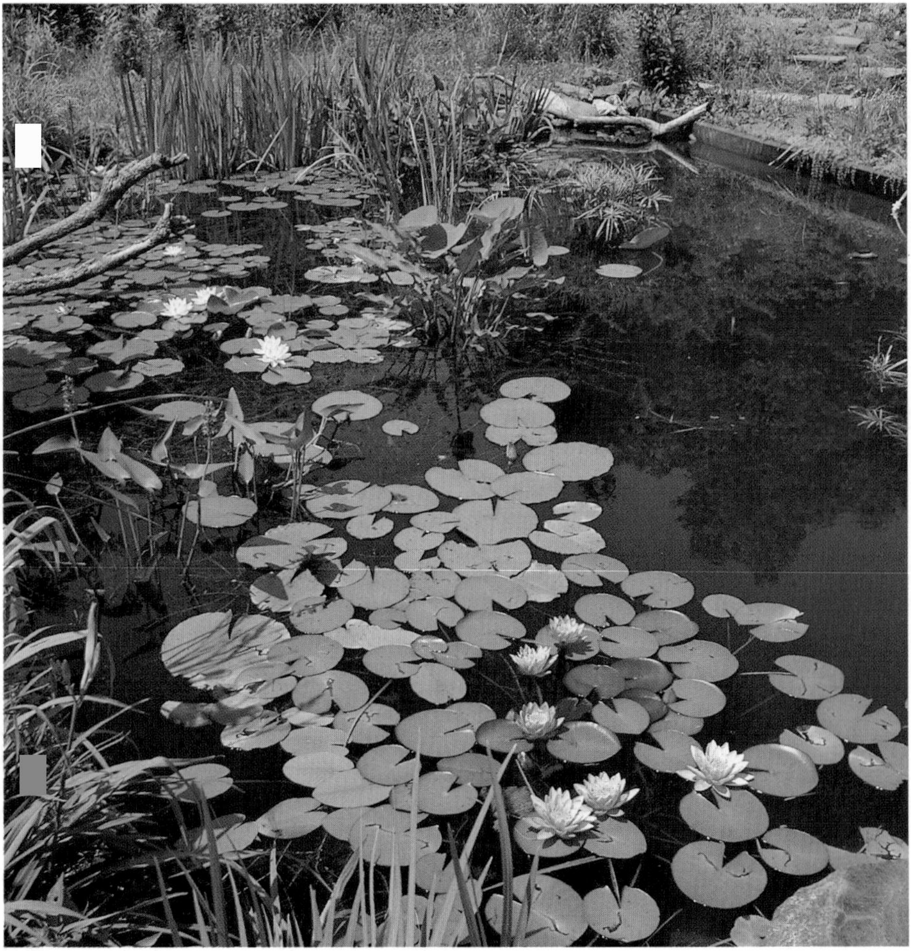

a pond!